Why T-shirts are co

Mary Schoeser

This book looks at the qualities of fabric made from cotton and polyester. It explains why fabrics amde from these yarns are particularly suitable for making t-shirts.

If you are using the book to find out particular facts about T-shirts or cotton, you do not have to read it all. Look at the **contents** (below) or the **index** (at the back) to find the best pages to help you. Then just read as much as you need to read.

The basic facts are given in big print, and more detailed information is in smaller print.

Contents

1 What is a T-shirt?	2
2 What are T-shirts made of?	4
3 Where does cotton come from?	6
4 Who wears cotton?	8
5 How is cotton worn?	10
6 Why are cotton clothes loose?	12
7 Why does cotton dry quickly?	14
8 Why is cotton mixed with polyester?	16
9 Why are T-shirts printed?	18
10 Why are T-shirts cotton?	20
Further information	22
Glossary	23
Index	24

1 What is a T-shirt?

A T-shirt is a piece of clothing that pulls on over your head. It usually has short sleeves and a round neck. It can be one colour, or have words or pictures printed on it.

If you think of the T-shirts that you, your friends and your family wear, you will know that T-shirts come in many sizes. They can also have lots of different patterns on them, but they all have some things in common. T-shirts are all the same, simple shape. They are machine-knitted, light in weight, and they are worn on their own in warm weather.

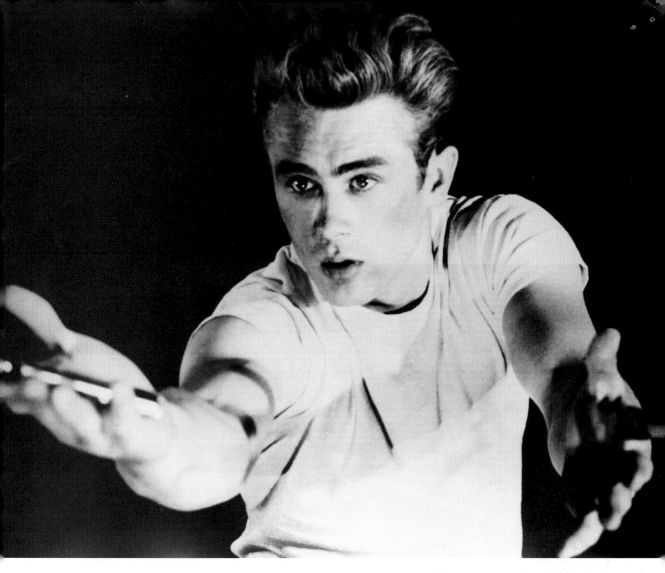

↑ In the 1950s T-shirts became fashionable to wear on their own. This is because they were worn that way by movie stars like James Dean.

How T-shirts got their name

A T-shirt got its name because of its simple shape. If you lay one of them out flat, you can see that it looks like the letter 'T'.

When T-shirts were first made, only men wore them. They wore them under shirts, so T-shirts were not made to fit closely because they were not meant to be seen. They began to be worn on their own in the 1950s, and then they were always plain white.

2 What are T-shirts made of?

T-shirts were first worn under a shirt or other garment. They had to be light in weight and easy to wash. They also had to be quick-drying. Cotton fabric does all these things.

The labels inside a T-shirt tell you what it is made from.

If you look at the labels inside your T-shirts, you will find that the most common ingredients are cotton and polyester.
The labels also tell you where the T-shirts are made and how you should wash them. There are laws which make the manufacturer include all this information on the labels.

⬆ White T-shirts can be washed in boiling water, but a coloured one cannot. This is because the colour will fade if it gets too hot when it is wet.

About labels

Sometimes the label will say '100% cotton', and this means that out of each 100 metres of fibre, 100 metres are cotton. In other words, '100% cotton' means it is all cotton. If cotton and polyester are both listed, the percentage is given for both materials, and the two percentages add up to 100.

3 Where does cotton come from?

Cotton comes from a vegetable plant. The fibres look like tiny hairs around the seed of the plant. It grows in tropical and hot areas of the world.

⬆ Cotton grows as very fine fibres. Their job is to keep the seeds in the centre from getting wet.

The cotton fibres vary in length from one centimetre to five centimetres. They can be twisted so that they make thread. This process is called spinning. For centuries India and Pakistan have been famous for the very delicate threads that were made by hand-spinners who lived in these countries.

⬆ Cotton is a short fibre, so it must be spun without jerking.
If it is not spun smoothly, it will be pulled apart.

Countries where cotton is grown

More than half the world's cotton crop is grown in the southern and western parts of the United States of America. Some other important countries for growing cotton are India, Pakistan and Egypt.

We know that cotton was grown a long time ago because old fabrics have been found. Fabrics woven from cotton over 5000 years ago have been found at Mohenjo-Daro, in the valley of the River Indus. Our word 'cotton' comes from the Arabic word 'qutn', or 'qutun'.

4 Who wears cotton?

Cotton has been worn for centuries in countries where the climate is warm or tropical. It was not worn very much in Britain until about 200 years ago.

Cotton was first worn in the places where it grew. The cotton plant was found growing along rivers, such as the Nile in Egypt or the Indus in India, because it needs both heat and water to grow. It was grown and worn in many other places, including Brazil, Peru, China, and Turkey.

⬆ Cotton garments were made like this in India.

⬆ Cotton growing along the Nile. In the past cotton had to be hand-picked.

This Indian palampore, or bedcover, was made of cotton and imported into England in the early 1700s. Only wealthy people could afford bedcovers like these.

Cotton inspired English inventors

Cotton has never grown in England, but imported Indian cottons inspired the English to master Indian ways of creating colours on cotton and to create machines to spin cotton.

Between 1769 and 1779 the Englishmen, James Hargreaves, Richard Arkwright, and Samuel Crompton each designed and made machines for spinning cotton. Soon after, the spinning, weaving and printing of cotton became one of the most important industries in England.

5 How is cotton worn?

Cotton is often worn in loose, simply-shaped garments. It makes a light-weight fabric, which is easy to tuck, fold, or wrap into place.

There are many traditional garments from around the world that are made of cotton. Some of them are very similar. Sarongs from Thailand and saris from India are both long, unshaped pieces of cloth. Similar garments are worn in Africa. The Yoruba men wear one called 'akwaja' meaning 'throw-over'.

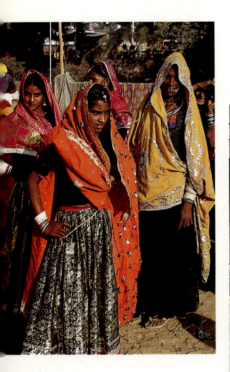

Many garments are made from a single length of cotton cloth. Often the cloth tells people which tribe, family or town the wearer comes from.

⬆ Kamez is the Indian word for T-shaped garments like these.

⬆ An Arab kaftan.

⬆ A simple dress.

'T' shaped garments

Caftans from the Middle East are among the many varieties of long-sleeved, long tunics worn around the world. A tunic is like a T-shirt, in that it is also 'T' shaped. Garments made in simple shapes like the T-shirt, tunic, or sari do not waste fabric. The shape is simple, so the cloth itself, or the images on it, become more important. The way that it is worn is also important.

6 Why are cotton clothes loose?

When it is hot, loose cotton clothes help to keep us cool. This is because cotton does not hold moisture. Instead it dries very quickly.

▲ A tight T-shirt is impractical, but it says something about the person who wears it.

Keeping clothes dry in a hot climate prevents the skin from feeling clammy. Tight cotton clothes stay in contact with the skin and make it slower to dry. T-shirts are still worn under shirts to protect them from perspiration. They need to be loose enough to let the perspiration dry quickly.

Air dries clothes

All clothes dry most quickly when they have air around them. This is why clothes are hung on a line or tumbled around in a drier. By wearing clothes that are loose, we allow air inside the garment to help keep it dry. Cotton is worn by many people who are active in warm weather, like tennis players and cricketers.

7 Why does cotton dry quickly?

Cotton fibres respond to moisture by moving. This exposes all of the damp surfaces to the air, and that is the reason why a cotton garment dries so quickly.

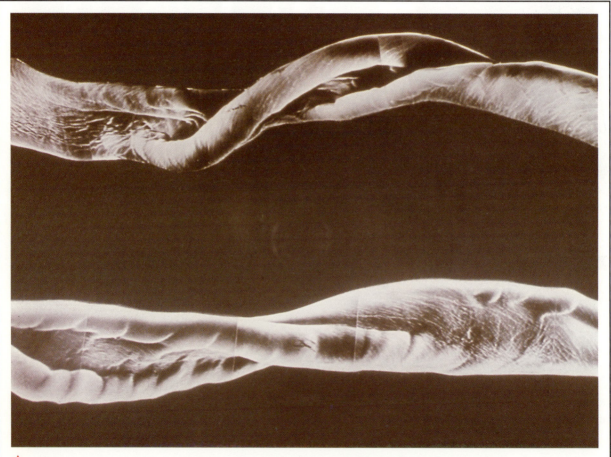

Under a microscope cotton fibres look like twisted ribbons with thickened edges.

We cannot see the cotton fibres moving, but because they are shaped like twisted ribbons, we can imagine them wriggling back and forth along their natural twist. The motion that cotton fibres make is very like that of a tiny tumble-drier.

 We use cotton towels because they dry quickly.

Comparing cotton with wool

We know that cotton dries quickly because we use tea-towels, flannels and bath towels that are made of cotton. If you take a cotton flannel and a piece of wool cloth of the same size and wet them both equally, you will find that the cotton flannel dries more quickly. This is because wool holds the water, and cotton does not.

8 Why is cotton mixed with polyester?

Cotton fibres move when they are wet. This makes them weak when they are wet. Mixing cotton with polyester, which is very strong, makes a fabric that lasts longer.

⬆ Polyester and cotton are often combined in items that need to be strong, easy to wash, and quick to dry. Lots of sheets and pillowcases are made of polyester and cotton.

Polyester yarn is made from chemicals that come from coal, air, water, and petroleum, and it has been available since 1946. It can be made to feel like cotton, and when it is combined with cotton, the result is a fabric that is stronger than cotton alone.

▲ Clothes made from polyester or from polyester and cotton are called 'wash and wear' because polyester does not crease. This means that the clothes seldom need ironing.

A way to test the strength of fabric

One of the tests that textile manufacturers use is called a 'rub test'. They use this test to find out the strength of a cloth by counting how many times it can be rubbed before it wears out. Cotton blended with polyester lasts much longer than cotton on its own. Dry cotton lasts longer than wet cotton.

▲ Canvas shoes like plimsolls wear through because they are woven from cotton. This happens even faster if the shoes are often wet.

9 Why are T-shirts printed?

All T-shirts are made from machine-knitted fabric. Knitting colours into the fabric makes the T-shirt more expensive, so colours are added on top of the finished cloth.

Solid-coloured T-shirts are also dyed after the cloth is made. In the last forty years there have been many improvements in the dyes for colouring cotton and polyester. Cotton is now easy to dye, and this means that you can colour your own T-shirt, although the colours may fade. T-shirts can be dipped in dye, or the dye can be painted on with a brush.

⬆ Screen printing by hand is one of the ways that designs are put on to T-shirts.

 These letters are stuck on top of the cloth.

About printing

Solid-coloured T-shirts are dipped in a vat of dye, but to make an image the T-shirt is usually printed. The image is created by using screens that let colour through in some places, but not in others.

When screen printing is used, the texture of the cloth stays the same. However, sometimes the image is heated and stuck on, and then you can feel the different texture of the stuck-on image. This is called transfer printing.

10 Why are T-shirts cotton?

T-shirts are worn to keep us cool and dry. We also like the words and images printed on them. Cotton dries fast and prints easily, so it is ideal for T-shirts.

Having started out as practical garments, T-shirts have become very fashionable. They have a simple shape, so they can be worn by everyone. They are made of cotton, or cotton and polyester, and this means that they can be worn all year round, under something when it is cold, and on their own when it is warm.

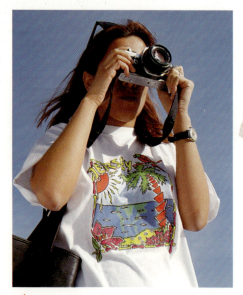

⬆ Holiday T-shirt

This T-shirt is hand-painted. ➡